POEMS ON STYLE
THE ART OF SHARING WHO YOU ARE

NIKKI VAN EKEREN

Copyright 2022 by Nikki Van Ekeren.
All rights reserved.

No part of this book may be used or reproduced in any manner whatsoever without written permission from the author, except for the use of brief quotations in a book review.

Your support of the author's rights is appreciated.

Cover art and layout by Matt Van Ekeren

Imprint: Independently published

For information regarding permission or distribution, contact nikkivanekeren@gmail.com

To discover more about the author visit nikkivanekeren.com

ISBN: 978-1-7355066-3-0

Reading a poem is a lot like looking at a painting. It touches something within and leaves everyone with a different feeling.

After reading this book, I hope you feel excited about who you are and honored to share your version of style. I hope that you continue to celebrate your body and enjoy the art of getting dressed everyday.

True beauty is having confidence in yourself and sharing this feeling with others.

chapter 1
inner peace creates outer style

1. inner peace creates outer style	11
2. permission to soar	13
3. put yourself out there more	15
4. learn how to celebrate yourself	17
5. develop your own style	19
6. let them see you	22
7. your style is a skill	24
8. own your vibe	27
9. to see the beauty	29
10. create your character	31
11. style is an attitude	33
12. to love oneself	35
13. to lighten up	37
14. your chosen path	40

chapter 2
the nuances of standing up for yourself

1. the nuances of standing up for yourself	45
2. a life well lived	46
3. style is never in a rush	48
4. the look of confidence	50
5. become your own style icon	53
6. continue to put yourself out there	55
7. your style strategy	57

8. keep it fresh	59
9. reach toward your dream life	61
10. grasping the essence of style	62
11. put yourself out there more	64
12. learning how to see yourself	66

chapter 3
the look of courage

1. the look of courage	71
2. walking with grace	72
3. the art of sharing who you are	75
4. unwavering sense of self	77
5. taking up space	80
6. be that person	81
7. on being called selfish	83
8. to blossom	86
9. enjoy it all	88
10. to be fully you, let the blame go	89
11. love. loving. loved.	91

chapter 4
it's that balance

1. it's that balance	97
2. proclaim what you want	99
3. fashion as a friend	100
4. style is unique, yet also learned	101

5. when you feel good — 104
6. the best days — 105
7. leveling up — 106
8. you've got this — 109
9. owning your worth — 110
10. imposter syndrome — 113
11. this is all about perseverance — 115
12. the tone of fashion — 116

chapter 5
learning who you are

1. learning who you are — 121
2. become your best friend again — 123
3. know your why — 125
4. gratitude is beauty — 126
5. inclusivity — 129
6. escaping the confines of the time — 131
7. love yourself first — 134
8. getting dressed — 135
9. your mood — 137
10. the movie in your mind — 139
11. your style does not belong to them — 140
12. the honor of being you — 142
13. live more and judge less — 144
14. lean into the discomfort — 146
15. living that dream life — 149

CHAPTER

01

Van Ekeren

INNER PEACE CREATES OUTER STYLE.

01

inner peace creates outer style

true beauty and style
lie within the ability
to connect
to your inner peace,
your inner certainty.

as you cultivate
this connection,
your style and confidence
develop new depths.

this inner knowing
acts as a magnet
luring you to experience
your best life.

you know who you are
and what works for you.
this connection
to yourself
helps you navigate through
the intense energies
of the external world.

Van Ekeren

> revel
> in your ability
> to create this inner peace.
> allow your style to reflect
> this inner strength.

02

permission to soar

if you thought you needed
permission
to soar,
you do not.
go out and do it.
emerge as your fullest self
and don't look back.

redefine what success means to you.
treasure your new definition of it.
meditate on it.

value what you choose worthy
and learn to not become distracted
by the temptations of the outside world.
let your inner world
be a safe haven,
a celebratory space
and a beautiful refuge
for you to thrive in.

bring this feeling with you
wherever you go.
know

Van Ekeren

that it is your time to soar
now
and
always.

03

put yourself out there more

the secret to happiness
is to just keep
putting yourself out there more
loving more
enjoying more
trying more
and not demanding anything
back from life
except for
exactly what it gives you.

Van Ekeren

**STYLE
IS A WAY TO
CELEBRATE
YOUR
LIFE ON
A DAILY BASIS.**

04

learn how to celebrate yourself

your personal style
should be a celebration
of you.

why not wake up
each day
with a desire
to exude your best self.

this does not mean
conforming
to society's definition of beauty.
it means
learning
what beauty means to you.
it means
celebrating
your life.
it means
putting your best self
out into the world.

style is a way
for others to see you.

Van Ekeren

it's also a lens
in which you can see yourself.

style is a way
to celebrate your life
on a daily basis.

05

develop your own style

as you engage
with the world around you,
observe
the style
the aesthetic
the beauty
and the space
you are in.
take notes
on what you like.
watch the people around you.
observe
who and
what you admire.

let this information
infuse you
from a pure place.
allow inner beauty
to transform
into outer style.

when you learn
to actively develop

your own personal style,

you discover that it's rooted in self compassion.

it's about cultivating

an authentic kindness toward

the art of beauty

and self expression.

style takes work.

style can be learned

and celebrated for an entire lifetime.

style doesn't have an expiration date.

learn to develop your own style

and revel in how confident

this makes you feel.

Poems on Style

**LET THEM SEE YOU
AS THE PERSON
YOU WANT TO BE.**

06

let them see you

let them see you
as the person you want to be.

you know who
this person is.

you've been working
on yourself,
now it's time to share
who you are.

let people see you.
let them have an opinion about you.

cultivate your character.
make decisions about who you want to be
before you enter a room.
lean into your ability to project confidence.

if you can read this poem,
you can become the person that
you
want
to be.

Poems on Style

you just have to
be honest with yourself
about who that is.
reach for this person.
work for it.
be it.

07

your style is a skill

learn to see
your
style
as a skill
that you can get better at
with practice.

what moves you?
who do you admire?

become clear
about what you like
and then work
to create it.

take comfort in how you
present yourself to the world.

style is contagious.
be courageous enough
to take on
your evolving style
as your own personal skill.

Poems on Style

embody it.
shine.
let others
begin to emulate you.

OWN YOUR VIBE.

08

own your vibe

timidity
is a learned response,
as is
boldness.

stand out.
become the version of you
who
enjoys
being seen.
let others comment
or have an opinion about you.
stand up tall
and proud
and never succumb.

if someone
has a negative reaction
toward your audacity,
they may secretly
wish to
exude that same
magical quality.
let them be.

Van Ekeren

      see them
      seeing you.
      own your vibe.
      learn how to stand out
      with genuine excitement
      for the art of life.

09

to see the beauty

remember
that beauty
is in the eye of the beholder.
so,
begin
beholding it
and seeing it.

merge wih it.
embody it.
create it.
share it.

redefine
what beauty means to you.

perhaps it means
taking care of yourself in new ways,
listening to yourself,
or exploring nature more often.
this new type of beauty may be found in how you
approach daily activities.
it may mean
taking more time to sip your morning coffee,

or staying home for the evening
or having a glass of wine
or giving yourself a compliment.

explore
what beauty means to you.
you will learn so much
about yourself.
you will discover
that you are actually
more beautiful
and fascinating
and exciting
than you had ever imagined.

lean into this.
tune into the beauty
that is always around you.
it is quiet
and bold.
see its nuances
and feel its glory.

10

create your character

decide who you want to be
and learn how to exude this character.

so often,
we become depressed
when we forget who we are
or when we covet another's life.

there is no better time
to emerge as your fullest self
than now.
learn about your heroes.
how did they act?
how did they dress?
how did they share their gifts?
go shopping for personality traits.
enjoy the process
and commit to it.
let it be fun.

you get to create and embody
the you
that you want to be.

**LEARN HOW
TO BE YOUR OWN
CHEERLEADER.**

11

style is an attitude

when you choose
to be seen,
you develop
the means in which to do so.
you learn
about yourself
in deep ways.
you enrich
this process of growth
by embracing the discomfort
that may arise
with being seen.
you are honest with yourself.

style is
about choosing to be bold.

when you decide
that you are not going to hide,
you will need to nourish yourself
in the right ways.
compliment others.
be there for others.

then,

do the same for yourself.

learn how to be

your own cheerleader.

smile more.

radiate.

feel the depth of your character

and channel it through

your style.

12

to love oneself

oscar wilde
said
"to love oneself
is the beginning
of a lifelong romance."

by loving yourself,
you choose to love
the one person
that can always love you back.

by loving yourself,
you are more eager
to try
to put forth the effort
and to evoke your true you-ness.

by loving yourself,
you can see clearly.
nothing fogs the view
more than self loathing.

to love oneself
creates an inner energy

that will never cease.
you are
the giver
and the receiver.
just by being you,
you can be more of you.
your abundant spirit
will always be pulsing through you.

13

to lighten up

when you
stop taking yourself so seriously,
you lighten up
and begin to enjoy life more.
you reach out to others
and truly enjoy
their company.
you can laugh
at the things
that used to haunt you.

when you lighten up,
you literally
feel lighter.
your mind is freer
your heart is open
and your body is safe.
you are not plagued
by irrational fears
created in the mind.
you are willing
to see
through the pain.

Van Ekeren

> to lighten up
> is to live more.
> your life
> will feel like your own work of art.
> you will see the poetry of life.
> you will radiate
> and be seen for the sparkle
> in your eye.

Poems on Style

**IT'S THE ENERGY
THAT YOU BRING
INTO YOUR LIFE.**

14

your chosen path

when you truly believe
that the path you're currently on
is your chosen path,
you have the eyes
to see the blessings
and possibilities
all around you.

you see how unique and special
you truly are
and that you're doing exactly
what you're supposed to.

you see how
it's not
the title,
the attention
or the accolades that matter,
it's the energy that you bring
into your life.

it is how you celebrate yourself
each day.
it's how you radiate

and infuse passion
into everything you do.
it is honoring the road that you're on
and knowing that it is
your chosen path.

CHAPTER

02

Van Ekeren

LEARN HOW TO STAND UP FOR YOURSELF IN YOUR OWN STYLE.

01

the nuances of standing up for yourself

you can smile
and be assertive.
you can be strong,
yet kind.
learn how to
stand up for yourself
in your own style.
being bold,
confident
and strong
are the roots
of personal style.

know who you are.

become comfortable
with your nuanced way of standing up for yourself.
do not be scared of anyone or anything.
generate confidence from within.
stand up
for yourself
in all circumstances.

02

a life well lived

when you nurture yourself
and your gifts,
you discover
how to truly live.
you learn the art
of self discipline,
yet have the courage
to share your shadow side.

life is full
of contradictions.
you are not fearful of this.
you strive
for a life well lived.

you understand
the magnitude
of this intention.
the beauty
and style
of a life well lived
will be your legacy.

Poems on Style

**STYLE IS NEVER
IN A RUSH.**

03

style is never in a rush

the marketing ploys
and social media campaigns
can fool anyone into thinking
that style is in a hurry.

one is pushed
to buy and consume
in order to stay relevant
and on trend.

yet,
style is never in a rush.

it is a way to visually share your essence.
it is an ongoing evolution.
style is a mood you radiate
wherever you go.
style is enjoyable
to its beholder.
style is nourishing
and invigorating.

style is fun.
it is something

Poems on Style

you love to share
and to witness.
let go of the needs
that others impose upon you
and discover
your own personal style.

04

the look of confidence

confidence
creates
the look.

that look,
that guides you through life
to meet your true destiny.
that look
that makes you feel good.

to exude this look,
discover what makes you feel confident.

step back
and learn about yourself.
what makes you feel good
about who you are?
how can you
stand up straight
and look people in the eye?
what makes you feel enigmatic?

discover
this essence within.

Poems on Style

you will learn

that you do not need to emulate

anyone else.

you have the skills

and ability

to create inner confidence.

Van Ekeren

BE YOUR OWN STYLE ICON.

05

become your own style icon

often
when we idolize another,
we see a part of ourself
in them.
we see our potential
being carried out
in their life.

is it the way
in which they carry themselves
in a crowded room?
is it how
they wear their clothes
with such confidence and power?
is it their boldness?

look to your
style icons
to become
your own.

if you can see
something you admire in another,
you can learn

how to integrate that
into your life and style.

learn how to observe
and learn
rather than covet
or judge.
if you like it,
try it.

become your own style icon.
be brave
and bold
in your aesthetic choices.
enjoy
putting yourself out there.

06

continue to put yourself out there

as we get
a bit too comfortable
in our current lifestyle,
we can forget to
push boundaries
and put ourselves out there.
it is vital
to continue to grow
and forge ahead.
doing so creates momentum
and positive forward motion.
continuing to put yourself out there
forces you
to not find solace
in solitary despair.
you learn
how to find the right people
by being the person
that you want to be.
this is a super power.
this ability
to go out into the wilderness
rather than retreat
will feed your soul.

Van Ekeren

**AS YOU CHANGE,
YOUR STYLE WILL
CHANGE.**

07

your style strategy

develop a strategy
to reflect your
evolving style.

throughout your beautiful years of life,
what works for you today
may not
work for you
tomorrow.
let this be a natural
and joyful thing.
embrace the fun
of change
and adapting to life.

be honest
with your evolution.
if you want to feel good
and look good,
let this be a priority.
learn what this means
to you now
and how you will evolve its meaning.
develop visual picture boards

and continue to add to them.
style is a visual art.
find a few widely known fashionable guides
to build your foundation upon.
be inspired by these people.
learn from them.

style is about evolving
and growing
and expressing yourself.
as you change,
your style will change.

by continuing to check in
with yourself,
you will forever be sharing your best self.

08

keep it fresh

if you find yourself
looking back with nostalgia,
strive to keep it fresh
in the present moment.
this may mean
experimenting with a new silhouette
or fashion combo.
this may mean
wearing your hair a different way.
admit to yourself
if you feel
stagnant
in your current look.
there is nothing
to be ashamed of.
reach for something
to freshen things up with.
it may be as easy
as choosing to smile.

**REACH TOWARD
YOUR DREAM
LIFE.**

09

reach toward your dream life

if you can envision it,
you can reach toward it.
allow your dream life
to come into complete focus.
see it.
reach toward it.
feel the style of it.
let the details emerge.
live as if you are in it.
see as if you are experiencing it.
reach toward your dream life
and feel it reaching back.

10

grasping the essence of style

the art of presenting yourself
to the world
is an honor.
it is not superficial
or selfish.
when you grasp the full essence of style,
you immediately become enraptured
in its significance.

how hard we work
to wrap a gift
or to choose a car
or to decorate a house.
these are hardly as special
as the style
in which you adorn yourself in.
your personal energy
and grace
are conveyed in your style.

rest into the enormity of it.
grasp the essence of style.
be transformed by the experience
and the honor of it all.

Poems on Style

it is not about appearing on trend
or of a particular look,
it is encapsulating your soul
in physical form.

11

put yourself out there more

rather than wait one more moment,
put yourself out there
now.

the act of putting yourself
out there more
is the road to happiness.

sure, this road
has no map
and may be bumpy
and frightening at times.
but, you have got to get out there.

do not think that you have to wait
until something happens
to be ready.
you are ready today.

it is your time
to put yourself out there.
create your own road map
as you forge ahead.

Poems on Style

DO THE INNER WORK.

12

learning how to see yourself

as you learn how to see yourself,
you learn how to carry
and present yourself.
this process unfolds
as you discover and celebrate
your value.

the eyes in which you view yourself
may be tinted
by those who came before you.
you may have to work hard
to see with clarity and kindness.
you may have to let go
of ancestral habits that have been passed down.

do the inner work.
learn more about yourself
and your unique beauty.

at first this process
will seem intense.
but, it will become more light and fun
as you discover how to integrate style
into the mix of it all.

Poems on Style

CHAPTER

03

Van Ekeren

WHEN YOU REACH FOR COURAGE, YOUR AESTHETIC NATURE CHANGES.

01

the look of courage

when you personify courage,
your aesthetic nature
changes.
you become
more confident,
more resilient
and more balanced.
you do not seek permission,
rather you seek to fulfill your purpose.
you know who you are
and your courage
radiates
from your being.

02

walking with grace

when you walk with grace,
you are embodying
the present moment.
you are not afraid
of what might be
or what you may be missing out on.
you are anchored into life
through your character
and self compassion.

you
merge
with grace.
you connect to your soul.

this inner connection
strengthens your other connections.
life seems vibrant.
you trust yourself
and those around you.
you are willing to try.

walking with grace
is an art form

that announces your presence.
embody grace
and let it be your guide.

THE ART OF SHARING WHO YOU ARE IS A CONTINUAL LESSON OF GROWTH, TRUST AND INTEGRITY.

03

the art of sharing who you are

when you share
your inner essence,
your external energy
heightens and elevates.
your generosity
is felt by yourself
and everyone that you come into contact with.
you let go
of the need to be seen in a certain way,
and just share
the you
that you are
right now.

the art of sharing who you are
is a continual lesson
of growth,
trust
and integrity.
you know
and inhabit your worth
while boldly sharing your heart.

it is a journey

of enforcing healthy boundaries.
it is giving
before you've received.
it is knowing who you are
so deeply
that it excites you
to share this truth.

04

unwavering sense of self

knowing who you are
is
knowing your inner poem,
your inner rhythm,
and feeling confident to share it.

that knowing
that connection
that inner essence
will be felt
by everyone you encounter.

when you possess this unwavering sense of self,
it lifts the energy
in the room.
it elevates your truth
and helps you be an advocate for
all truth seekers.

this inner knowing
is a skill
is an art
is a type of poetry
that takes time to develop.

it will nurture
your ability to love generously,
yet flex your ability to enforce boundaries.
loving
does not mean
being taken advantage of.

you will instinctually know
how to stand up for yourself,
how to share your voice
and how to pursue the right opportunities.

Poems on Style

IT IS TIME TO TAKE UP SPACE.

05

taking up space

there may come a time
in your life,
when you
want to become invisible.
this feeling could
be a literal
or a metaphorical stance.
it could have emerged
to please others,
to gain love
or to abide to a cultural code of conduct.

it is time to stop
fading away.
it is time to
take up space.

proclaim who you are
physically and energetically.
be seen.
see yourself.
there is no need to hide,
share your essence freely and willingly.

06

be that person

have you
ever looked up to a person
who was so jovial
and proud
of who they were?
you were in awe
of their magnitude.
you loved being in their presence.
just by being near them,
you felt elevated.

go,
be that person.

embody that amount of self love.
send out ripples of happy energy
to all.
enjoy being you
and do not be afraid to tell others.
be the example to another
on how to radiate
your fullest essence

Van Ekeren

IF THEY CALL YOU SELFISH, SO BE IT.

07

on being called selfish

what definition
are we referring to
when we think of the word,
selfish?
why are we so scared
to be called by this term?

it is time to
stop,
pause
and let this fear go.

take up space.
own your voice.
speak up.
honor yourself and your needs first
and then share your leftover resources
with others.
let go
of the fear
of
the word,
selfish.

Van Ekeren

you must take care of yourself
before you can have fun,
before you can create,
before you can love,
before you can do anything of value.
be connected to yourself.
if they call you selfish,
so be it.

TO BLOSSOM IS TO TRULY EMBODY YOUR SMILE.

08

to blossom

to blossom is to become
the person
that you joyfully
and continually create.
you know that your happiness
begins on the inside,
so you are learning
how to create this feeling.

to blossom is to trust in yourself completely.
it is that unwavering connection
you have cultivated
from years of practice.
you trust yourself
because you refuse to let yourself down.

to blossom is to exude unconditional love.
you know that this form of self compassion
is abundant;
therefore you feel loved
at all times.
this act is not contingent on anything external,
it is a gift you bestow upon yourself.

to blossom is to share your essence with the world.
just as the butterfly opens up its wings
to reveal a beautiful image,
you begin to share your unique style
with the world.
you enjoy the art of being seen
and honor this process.

to blossom is to truly embody your smile.
you understand how powerful
this gesture
can be,
so you lovingly share it.

09

enjoy it all

rather than pretend to know it all,
just enjoy it all.
be honest about what you are working on
and enjoy the process.
life is about
becoming,
not arriving.
continue to grow
while bestowing grace upon yourself
and those around you.
life is meant to be lived
with gratitude
and joy.

10

to be fully you, let the blame go

you probably have been hurt
by someone
in the past.
you may have reason
to blame them
for your lack of boldness
or confidence.
how do you get past this mental roadblock
and free up your energetic energy?

let the blame go.

try to completely accept the past
and learn from it.
discover how to
focus your mental energy
on what you can control,
rather than on what
you have no control over.
the past happened,
so your present self
could emerge.

honor your story.

honor your pain
and inclination to blame.
accept it.
then,
work on it.

let the blame go
to be the fullest version of yourself.
let the blame go
so you can shine.

11

love. loving. loved.

if your life
is based on the act of loving,
you will be able to heal
from anything.
nothing is too painful
or traumatic
to be able to put the pieces back together.
you love.
you are loving.
you are loved.
you feel it.
you share it.
you receive it.
it is a beautiful life
when you know that love
is the driving force.
sure, there are bad people
who may seem to be thriving,
but do not spend your time
observing them.
love yourself.
love your work.
invest your precious gift of time
on you and your projects,

Van Ekeren

       your work,
       your style
       and your value.
       you will never run out of love
       to feel
       or to share.

Poems on Style

CHAPTER

04

EMOTIONAL HYGIENE IS THE EPITOME OF STYLE.

01

it's that balance

emotional hygiene
begins
with balance.
this state of equilibrium
is achieved through
accepting our truth,
living in this truth
and letting it emerge as integrity.

having emotional hygiene
is all about honesty.
being real enough
with yourself
to admit your vulnerabilities
and to honor them.

it takes work
and dedication.
it involves making new habits
and letting some go.

emotional hygiene
is rooted in
kindness and compassion.

it is about having the courage to share
what is in your heart.

emotional hygiene
is the epitome of style.
when you are compassionate
toward yourself and others,
you will always be on trend.

02

proclaim what you want

if you never
want to
feel jealousy again
or covet another's lifestyle,
proclaim what you want
and work for it.
be honest with yourself.

be truthful
about what you really want
and the work that is required to get it.
invest in yourself.
keep on keeping on.

the act of persistency
for yourself
for your goals
for your wants
is nourishing and fulfilling.
the work
works.
the work
feels good.
go get what you want.

03

fashion as a friend

fashion
as a friend.
it molds to your moods
and is always ready to make a statement.
it is the perfect partner
in the tumultuous journey of life.

fashion
as a beacon of hope
for when you feel alone.
it is that friend that reaches out to you
and reminds you that you are special.

fashion
as a metaphor to remember
the art of nonconformity.
you do not need to conform
in your fashion choices.
be bold and show the world who you are.

fashion
as a fun form of self expression.
continue to push boundaries
and remember to have fun with it.

04

style is unique, yet also learned

as you evolve and discover
what makes you feel like you,
your style will take new shapes.
perhaps,
the key accessories will stay the same,
but your overall energetic feeling
will continue to grow,
enhance
and mature.

your joyful experiences
and aesthetic eye
will draw you to new ideas.
you will be able to combine different influences
in new and exciting ways.
you will feel the nuances
that a subtle blazer
or shoe
or necklace
can bring to an outfit.
you will embody the fun
of gathering new additions
to your wardrobe.

Van Ekeren

your style will grow
alongside of you.
you will view your clothing and accessories
as beautiful art pieces that you have the honor
of wearing on a daily basis.

Poems on Style

**HAVE FUN
WITH IT.**

05

when you feel good

when you feel good,
you are more likely to share this side of you
with others.
you may smile more
and encourage another.
you may even find yourself
enjoying small talk
in the elevator
or at your local coffee shop.

the goal is to feel good.
develop your ability to understand
what this means to you.

feeling good
does not have to be a serious endeavor.
it can be joyful and nourishing
at the same time.

06

the best days

the best days
are when you ease up
and enjoy life.
when you trust yourself
and understand
that life presents challenges.
when you do not judge yourself or others.
when you choose to know
and to embody
your best self.
when you know that you can handle anything.
when you do not let fearful intrusive thoughts
bully you.
when you see everything and everyone
as an equal.
the best days
are everyday
that you truly see yourself
and honor your story.

07

leveling up

confidence,
beauty,
and boldness
emerge
when you merge with your truth.
essentially,
you level up.
you pronounce who you are.
you do not hide from anything.

how does one get here?

practice.
commitment.
honesty.
leveling up is a continual gift
to give yourself.
it will enhance your inner
and outer connections.
enjoy the process
and savor sharing your best self.

Poems on Style

**BEAUTY IS
CONFIDENCE
IN ONESELF.**

Van Ekeren

YOU'VE GOT THIS.

08

you've got this

the serene calling
that comes from within
that reminds you
of your strength
is a form of beauty.
it ignites your inner flame of courage
and signals your mind to take charge.
beauty is confidence
in oneself.
fall into the power of this statement.
let it change you.
your most fabulous self
is only one thought away.
you've got this.
summon the strength to simultaneously call and
be called
to flex your inner confidence.
this is an
act of beauty.

09

owning your worth

don't wait for someone
to tell you
that you're worthy,
own your worth.
don't seek out legitimacy
from external sources,
own your essence.

the best feeling
doesn't come from owning something external,
it comes from owning
your voice,
your story
and your style.

embrace the art of self expression.
hear your own voice
before you seek another's approval
or acceptance.
share your personal style
with boldness.
let go of trying to impress anyone,
it's never been fulfilling.

Poems on Style

work hard to practice the art of
joyful self expression.
celebrate yourself.

maybe when one longs
to be understood or heard,
one needs to hear
themself
more clearly.

own your worth
and define it as is you grow.

**IF YOU SEEK
TO BE A CERTAIN
PERSON,
GO BE
MORE LIKE IT.**

10

imposter syndrome

when you hear
an inner voice
accuse you of being an imposter,
this your cue
to develop an inner mantra.
form a short sentence to habitually recite
when you feel the twinge of being an imposter.

the feeling of imposter syndrome
is your mind
actually trying to protect you.
when you navigate toward
heightened experiences,
there's something inside everyone
that tries to protect you from the unknown.
when you are in pursuit of your dreams.
this protective mechanism gets louder.

remember to keep going
to continue creating
and to keep forging ahead.
remember your mantra
and recite it to yourself.
rely on this mantra to

remind you of your value.
become indifferent to the hurtful vibe
of the feeling of being an imposter.
it is an irrational fear
trying to keep you small and safe.

if you seek to be a certain person,
go be more like it.
do not let the inner critic
intimidate you.

11

this is all about perseverance

life all about learning
and practicing
and then learning more.
it is all about living with purpose
and focus
and determination.
your energy
and style
reflect your confidence
and ability to persevere.
continue to work on your inner
and outer appearance.
keep the momentum of self love flowing.
the art of how you present yourself
to the world matters.
honor this element of self growth
and understand its metaphorical significance.

12

the tone of fashion

bright
beautiful
bold
shades of energy
ripple from you
when you are happy
to be you.
you feel good in your mind
and in your body.

the tone of your fashion choices
communicates your message
of self love and compassion
when you confidently stride into any room.

you feel happy
to be you
when you have accepted
your gifts and talents
and choose to share them with the world.

you celebrate yourself
through your fashion.
its tonality sings your beautiful song.

Poems on Style

it's an inner beauty
that translates to the outer part of you.

you thoroughly enjoy life
when you are your true self
and feel happy to express it.
sing your beautiful inner song
through your fashion.

CHAPTER

05

Van Ekeren

WHAT MAKES YOU, YOU?

01

learning who you are

the journey
of discovering who you are
begins with a desire
to go deeper
and to explore
your truth.

what makes you
you?
how do you want
to express yourself?
how do you see yourself?

learning who you are
is a continual process.
your style will reflect
this monumental awareness.

so, dig a little deeper
and reach toward
your inner truth.
face the insecurities
that were projected onto you.
by shining a light on this pain,

Van Ekeren

you can help distinguish its grasp on you.

your pure nature
can become hidden by
another's shadow.
seize back
your essence,
your beauty
and your story.

02

become your best friend again

because the
best style
comes from
within.
it comes from
knowing
that you can trust yourself.

when you become
your
best friend again,
you awaken
something inside.
you
ignite
that inner spark.

it is that
certain something
that happy and vibrant
and stylish people
exude.
it is self love.

Van Ekeren

KNOW YOUR WHY.

03

know your why

when you know
your "why"
you know your purpose.
you know why
you create what you do
and your work feels meaningful.
you are not as easily distracted
by temporary attention or accolades.

when you know
your "why"
you are not thrown off course
if others do not applaud your work.
life just feels more nourishing
and fun
when you know your purpose.

04

gratitude is beauty

when you feel grateful,
you feel the purity of love.
you connect with
the warmth of life
and feel safe.

this truth
radiates an inner beauty,
a magnetic force,
that attracts you
to where you need to be.

gratitude is a graceful beauty
that is accessible
to all who reach for it.

it lies within you at all times.
try to rely on it
when you feel triggered
or fearful.

try to think
in the beautiful shades of gratitude,
and let this process

Poems on Style

change the chemical makeup of your mind.
it will bring you to new frontiers
that you never dreamed possible.
it will nourish your soul
with the purest energy
one can experience.

Van Ekeren

**LET'S CELEBRATE
THE INCLUSIVITY
OF BEAUTY.**

05

inclusivity

sometimes it seems as if
the idea of
beauty
has been manipulated
and manufactured
to appear out of reach.

it is time
to take back
the idea of beauty.
it is time
to invite everyone into the conversation.

let's celebrate
the inclusivity
of beauty.
let's choose
how we feel about ourselves
and not allow others
to dictate
this monumental act.

beauty
is within.

it is how we treat ourselves
and one another.
it is our energetic footprint,
our essence
and our contributions.

06

escaping the confines of the time

each moment in time
has a societal pull
on those who live
within it.
we all inherently want to fit in.
we want to be a part of the group.
this is a human desire
and nothing to feel bothered by.

it is when we act in the best interest
of how others see us
that we begin to be confined,
constricted
and stifled.
our need to be seen in a certain way
becomes the defining characteristic
of who we are.

the first way to navigate through
this inevitable path
is to be aware of it.
acknowledge your human nature.
honor it.
then, learn how to work through it.

you can become mentally stronger
when you work at it.
your desire to rise up
and work toward your dreams
can define you.
your ability to persevere
and not be distracted by the trends of the time
will sustain you.

**LOVE YOURSELF
FIRST AND
KNOW THAT YOU
ARE ENOUGH.**

07

love yourself first

to truly love others,
you must love yourself first.
this inner feeling
that you shower yourself with
is a gift
that you can learn how to continually bestow.
it is always attainable.
it is always within reach.
trust that you've got the ability
to unconditionally love yourself.
believe that you are capable of this great love.
discover how this act
will set an energetic base within
that guides you to your most fabulous life.
love yourself first
and know that you are enough.

08

getting dressed

getting dressed
should be
the best part of your day.
it's that moment when
you get to choose
how you present yourself to the world.

you get to peruse
your beautifully curated closet
that consists of pieces
you've bought for yourself.
it's a daily reminder
of self care
and passion.
each article of clothing
that hangs in your closet
conjures up a memory
of why and how
you purchased it.
you love the energy
that your closet shares with you.

as you create
the right outfit for today,

Van Ekeren

your mood of the moment
is boldly conveyed.
you see yourself
and look forward to sharing who you are
with the world.

getting dressed allows you
to tell the story
of who you are
today
as your inner strength
bursts through.

09

your mood

you are the one
who sets your mood.
you are the one
continuously writing your story
and then sharing it with others.

how do you describe yourself?
how do you tell your story?
are you the victim or the victor?

these narratives are up to you.
you set the tone
and the entire vibe
of your mood.
you get to write
and rewrite
your story.

work hard at
becoming the version of you
that you want to be.

**CULTIVATE
THE SKILLS TO
STYLISTICALLY
SHINE.**

10

the movie in your mind

you get to write
the movie in your mind.
you get to replay
the good
or the bad.
which will you choose?
this moment by moment choice
is entirely up to you.

your mental movie
will support the
thesis you create about yourself.
craft this beautiful mantra
with the utmost of care.

create the movie in your mind
that you want to see.
be the star of your own show.
cultivate the skills to stylistically shine.
craft the inner charisma
and charm
that feels good to exude.

11

your style does not belong to them

have you ever
thought
about how the idea of ownership
plays into style?
do you feel that your style
is truly yours?
or do you feel as if
your personal influences are projected onto you?

your style does not belong to them,
it belongs to you.

if you ever feel disconnected from this truth,
revisit your definition of the word
style.
what does it mean to you?
what is your relationship with it?

remember that you get to choose
what you think is beautiful and
what is not.
you do not have to be told
what beauty is.

Poems on Style

take back ownership
of the word, style.
let it harmonize with your
inner song.
sing as loudly and boldly
as you can.

12

the honor of being you

simply put,
you get to be you.
your grace,
grit,
style
and essence
are yours
to share.
what an honor.
what a gift.
live knowing this truth
and share your presence
and style
with those worthy of appreciating it.

Poems on Style

**LIVE MORE.
JUDGE LESS.**

13

live more and judge less

perhaps,
we start judging
when we stop participating.

let go,
have fun,
laugh,
participate,
get up and do something.

don't let your fear
hold you back
from living
your life.

go
live
today.

jump into the newness,
the changing times,
and the joy that comes
with living openly.

live more,
judge less.
open up your mind
to the possibilities out there.

14

lean into the discomfort

when you realize
how much of your life has been spent
running from discomfort,
you begin to understand the power
of leaning into it.
the amount of time and energy
that you have exuded to avoid
that conversation or person
now astounds you.
you would rather spend this time
confronting said person or situation
and then moving on with your beautiful life.

there will always be discomfort in life.

you can either
run from it
or acknowledge it
and lean into it.
the discomfort is
and will always be there.
it is human nature
to want to protect yourself.
honor your tendencies,

Poems on Style

while working on them.
you will feel buoyant,
bold
and powerful
when you lean
into
the discomfort.

Van Ekeren

YOUR DREAM LIFE IS WITHIN YOU NOW.

15

living that dream life

when you remember to
redefine what
love,
success
and happiness
truly mean to you,
you realize that you
have more control than you think.
your dream life
is within you now.
you can project your joy outward
and not fear the future.
your state of mind
is yours.
no one can take it away from you.
live that dream life
now
and enjoy it.

Van Ekeren

About the Author

Nikki Van Ekeren is a writer and an artist. Her style of poetry is rooted in optimism, self growth, stoicism and an appreciation for nature.

She is fascinated with the process of inner discovery and learning how to empower oneself.

Her other poetry books include *Grace & Grit*, *These Poems Are About Sunny Days*, *Palm Trees and Possibilities*, and for children, *You Get to Be You*.

www.ingramcontent.com/pod-product-compliance
Lightning Source LLC
Chambersburg PA
CBHW071244070526
44583CB00017B/2322